10003888001

DATE DUE

D0573751

THE RATTLE
AND
THE DRUM

THE RATTLE AND THE DRUM

NATIVE AMERICAN RITUALS AND CELEBRATIONS

BY LISA SITA

ILLUSTRATED BY
JAMES WATLING

THE MILLBROOK PRESS
BROOKFIELD,
CONNECTICUT

Library of Congress Cataloging-in-Publication Data
Sita, Lisa, 1962–
The rattle and the drum : Native American rituals
and celebrations / by Lisa Sita.
p.   cm.
Includes bibliographical references and index.
Summary: Explores the rich and colorful variety of
Native American ceremonies and celebrations—everyday
rituals, initiation ceremonies, rituals to heal the sick
and celebrate the changing seasons, and powwows that
forge ties between different Native groups. Instruc-
tions for games, crafts, and recipes provide readers
with "hands-on" activities related to the text.
ISBN 1-56294-420-7 (lib. bdg.)
1. Indians of North America—Rites and ceremonies
—Juvenile literature.   I. Title.
E98.R3S46   1994
299'.7—dc20   93-27209   CIP   AC

Published by The Millbrook Press
2 Old New Milford Road
Brookfield, Connecticut 06804

Copyright © 1994 by Lisa Sita
Illustrations copyright © 1994 by James Watling
All rights reserved
Printed in the United States of America
1   3   5   2   4

E
98
R3
S46
1994
J

CONTENTS

THE RATTLE
AND
THE DRUM

CHAPTER ONE

---□---

RITUALS AND CELEBRATIONS

When you visit a powwow, you enter a world of lively music and dance, bright color, and warm feeling. The drum is the heartbeat of this festive celebration, and the sound of the rattle carries the spirit of many of its dances.

All across North America, Native American peoples have created independent nations with rich and varied ways of life. Each nation has developed its own language, customs, beliefs, and traditions. A powwow is a social celebration that brings different groups together and strengthens their ties. It is a time when dancers match their skills, when artists and craftspeople display their work, and when Native musicians and storytellers share their talents. Most powwows are open to the public, too.

The drum and the rattle also play an important part in many of the events expressing the religious traditions that Native Americans especially value. These sacred rituals and ceremonies include powerful songs, poetic prayers, and beautiful dances.

What is a ritual? A ritual is a set of actions that follow the same pattern, usually for a special event or reason. For example, dressing up as a witch or a ghost on Halloween and ringing the neighbors' doorbells for "trick or treat" is a ritual of sorts. Most rituals are related to religious and spiritual beliefs. For us Halloween is like a game, but many centuries ago it was an important religious event honoring the sun god and the lord of the dead. Religious rituals are sacred, which means they deserve the highest respect.

Religious rituals are often part of a larger ceremony involving many people joined together in prayer. The ceremony may celebrate a happy personal occasion, such as a birth or marriage, or it may mark a crisis, such as an illness or death. It may also deal with a community concern, such as the need for rain or for making peace with another group. Most Native American rituals and ceremonies include singing and dancing as a way of praying to the spirits and to the Creator. Each Native group has a name for the Creator in its own language. For some the Creator is a specific supernatural being; for others, a powerful force that takes many forms and dwells in all living things.

All Native peoples agree that humans, along with the animals and the plants of the earth, form part of a greater world that includes powers and forces we cannot usually see. They believe that these powers and forces are as real as we are. Spirits and supernatural beings are never very far away, and the people may call on them for help and guidance. The spirits and supernatural beings sometimes appear to people in visions or dreams. They can appear as animals, as people, or in a

form all their own, like the False Faces of the Iroquois or the kachinas of the Pueblo societies.

To Native Americans the natural world and the supernatural world are two sides of the same coin. The natural world, which can be experienced with the five senses, and the supernatural world, which can be experienced through faith and prayer, are not separate but connected. Together they form a whole—the world in which all things, natural and supernatural, live. Native Americans believe it is important to recognize and respect both worlds.

In ancient times, long before any living person can remember, the spirits and supernatural beings appeared to the people and spoke, instructing them in the proper ways to pray and give thanks. These became the rituals and ceremonies that are practiced today as they have been for centuries. Although both the natural and supernatural worlds are always present, rituals and ceremonies bring the two worlds closer together. Native Americans believe that on such occasions human beings can communicate clearly with the spirit world because the spirits are then present among the people.

There are several types of rituals and ceremonies. Some are everyday rituals. Others are seasonal. There are rituals to heal a sick or suffering person, and rituals that allow a person to move from one stage of life into another.

Each Native society has its unique way of celebrating life, of reaching out to the supernatural world, and of continuing the traditions of its ancestors. This book explores a small part of the many rituals and festivals of Native America.

CHAPTER TWO

---◉---

INITIATION CEREMONIES

All people are born into this world and experience the same stages of life—childhood, adulthood, and old age—before leaving it. As a person goes through this life cycle, many important personal changes will take place. Like people in all societies, Native Americans have rituals to recognize these changes. These include rituals for birth and death, for the naming of a child, and for marriage. Another important ritual takes place when a person changes his or her role in the community. This event is known as initiation, and the person is called the initiate.

Some initiation rituals occur when a person moves from childhood into adulthood. This usually takes place at the age of puberty (about twelve to fourteen years old), the time when a boy's or girl's body begins to physically change into that of a man or woman. Other initiation rituals celebrate a person's entry into a secret society. This is a kind of graduation ceremony.

An initiation ritual usually forms part of a larger ceremony. It is a time when the community gathers together to witness important changes in someone's life and to honor the person or people being initiated.

THE GIRLS' PUBERTY RITE OF THE APACHE

Traditionally, Native American women have been well respected within their societies. Women give birth to children, and so they are creators of life. Because they allow the future generations of the group to exist, women are greatly valued.

In New Mexico an Apache girl who reaches puberty is honored with a four-day ceremony. Many friends and visitors come to the event to celebrate her progress from girl to woman.

On the first day a ritual shelter is made of four spruce saplings. A buckskin is laid on the ground within it for the girl to dance on during the ceremony. Traditionally, she would wear a buckskin dress, dyed yellow to represent corn pollen. Today a girl may wear either buckskin or a yellow cloth dress. An older woman is chosen as godmother. This woman will be the girl's attendant during the ceremony.

Throughout the ceremony the girl must behave in a proper and careful way. She is believed to have the power during this time to cure people by touching them. As the sick come to her for aid, she receives them. She represents the supernatural being White Painted Woman, who first brought this ritual to the Apache. She must think positive thoughts about her future. If the ceremony goes well, she will have a good life and will be a good, responsible woman, a role model for other young girls.

As night falls on each of the four days, a bonfire is lit and more dancing takes place. Visitors perform the social dances called round dances. Especially moving are performances of another type of dance, the Mountain Spirit Dance. Here the dancers represent the *gan*, spirits that live in the sacred mountains. They move and gesture in the firelight wearing traditional fringed clothing, hoods of buckskin, and tall painted headdresses. Their bodies are painted with symbols.

It is said that the *gan* once lived among the Apache. But because they did not wish to die, they left to find a world where life never ends. By performing the role of the *gan*, the Apache dancers drive away sickness and misfortune and bring blessings to the ceremony.

At the end of the four days the shelter is taken down and the guests leave the ceremonial grounds. The girl and her family remain there until the ninth day, when she is purified in a bath of suds made from the yucca plant. The initiation ceremony is now over, and the girl has become a woman of the Apache nation.

THE HAMATSA SOCIETY OF THE KWAKIUTL

Many Native American nations have secret societies. Their members have certain kinds of knowledge that is not available to other members of the community. Usually this knowledge has to do with the world of the supernatural. For the Kwakiutl of Vancouver Island and coastal British Columbia, one of the most important secret societies is the Hamatsa.

The misty forests of the Northwest Pacific Coast have always supplied a wealth of wood and other natural resources. Native peoples of the area have used the forest resources to create objects of great beauty. These include carved wooden boxes made for storage and for use as cooking pots, elaborate masks painted and decorated with cedar bark, and towering totem poles made from whole cedar trees.

Traditionally, a person's standing in the community depended on his wealth and importance. But the Kwakiutl measure wealth not only in how much material goods a person or family owns. Families also own the right to perform certain songs, dances, and stories, which often tell about encounters between a family's ancestors and supernatural beings.

Families used to live in large plank houses along the beach. Each village had several chiefs. To mark an important event such as a marriage, a death, or the raising of a totem pole, a chief would host a ceremony called a potlatch. This ceremony is still an important part of Kwakiutl life. It includes feasting, speeches, the performance of dance dramas, and the giving of gifts to all the guests present. In the past this elaborate ceremony lasted four days and tremendous amounts of blankets, bowls, food, and other items were given away. Today the ceremony usually lasts only a single day. Gifts are still given to the guests, but now these might include plasticware, electric blankets, and nonstick cookware.

The potlatch is also the time for a person to be initiated into the Hamatsa Society. The Kwakiutl say that sometimes supernatural beings possess humans and cause them to act in unusual ways. One of the most important supernatural beings is the Cannibal. He lives in the mountains at the North End of the World in a house whose chimney always has red smoke rising from it. Only people whose family members have been possessed from generation to generation by the Cannibal may be initiated into the Hamatsa Society.

In the past a boy or, occasionally, a girl who was to be initiated into the Hamatsa Society would leave the village and spend up to four months living in the woods. There, it is told, he would be possessed by the Cannibal and grow wild. Actually, the initiate would be living there with older Hamatsa Society members, learning the Hamatsa dances and his new responsibilities as a member of the society. Upon returning to his village, he was ready to take part in the initiation ritual.

Today, initiates no longer spend time in the woods. The ritual, like the potlatch at which it is held, lasts one evening instead of four. It begins with the sound of whistles, which seems to be coming from all directions. Then an older Hamatsa member approaches the initiate and puts a ring of cedar bark around his neck. The initiate then begins to act untamed and ferocious, dancing about and calling out. Because he is supposed to be possessed by the Cannibal, he may rush up to people and act as if he were going to bite them. Attendants at the dance hold him by the arms and try to calm him.

The initiate continues to act wild, crouching down and then jumping up, his arms out, his hands shaking. As the dance progresses, he becomes more calm, helped by a female dancer who is one of his close relatives. Other dancers enter wearing huge, brightly painted carved masks with large beaks representing supernatural birds. Finally, during the last part of the dance, the initiate becomes completely tame and wears a special garment to show that he is once again a regular member of the community. As the ritual ends he is a member of the Hamatsa Society.

CHAPTER THREE

---◉---

EVERYDAY RITUALS

All Native American peoples have "everyday rituals." *Everyday* means that they may be conducted at any time of the day or night, on any day of the year, and as often as a person feels moved to do them.

---◉---

TOBACCO OFFERINGS AND SWEAT RITUALS OF THE LAKOTA

In the Black Hills of South Dakota is a mountain called Bear Butte that looks like a bear sleeping on its stomach. Bear Butte, like the entire Black Hills area, has always been a sacred place to the Lakota and Cheyenne peoples. It is a place of peace and solitude. The spirits are said to be present here, and so people still come to the butte to pray.

Today Bear Butte is also a national park where hikers go to walk its trails. During the summer months the trails are surrounded by plants, colorful flowers, and trees. The air is fragrant with the scent of pine. All around are the sounds of birds, buzzing insects, and the rustle of leaves in the breeze.

A plant with silvery-white leaves grows in clumps beside the trails. This is sage. People of the Plains nations consider this plant to be a natural cleanser. They use it to purify people and objects. Sacred objects are stored with sage to protect them from being contaminated. People also burn sage so that the smoke can cleanse the air. Other plants that are burned are sweet grass and cedar tips. Many Native peoples across North America today burn these plants.

One of the trails on Bear Butte is known as the ceremonial trail. It is different from other hiking trails: All around, hanging from tree branches, are strips of colored cloth. Some of the strips of cloth are long, some short, some just little pieces—but all of them have bulging pinches of tobacco wrapped in them. The cloth and tobacco were tied to the trees by people who came here to pray.

The tobacco plant is native to the Americas. It is said that the spirits enjoy tobacco, as some humans do. For this reason many Native peoples throughout the continent offer tobacco as gifts to the spirits when they pray. Sometimes people tie the tobacco in cloth, sometimes they sprinkle it on the ground, and sometimes they burn it. Farming peoples may offer corn pollen or cornmeal as well as tobacco. Like burning sage, sweet grass, and cedar, making an offering of corn or tobacco to the spirits is one of the everyday rituals that many Native nations have in common.

Tobacco is also offered by smoking it in a pipe. On the Plains, pipes usually have a red stone bowl and a long wooden stem, sometimes beautifully decorated with carvings, beadwork, or porcupine quillwork.

These pipes are sacred and powerful objects that must be smoked with respect and good thoughts.

The Lakota tell us that it was a spirit, White Buffalo Calf Woman, who brought the first pipe to their people. White Buffalo Calf Woman appeared to two warriors who were out hunting. As she approached them she kept changing from a beautiful woman to a buffalo and back again to a woman. Realizing they were seeing a sacred being, the warriors were awed. But when one of them tried to touch her, she turned him into a pile of snake-infested bones. She told the second warrior to return to his people. They were to prepare for her arrival by setting up a special tepee.

When White Buffalo Calf Woman arrived at the warriors' camp, she presented the first pipe to their leader. She told the people that they were to use the pipe in prayer. She also instructed them in how to conduct seven sacred rituals in which the pipe should be used.

One of the seven rituals is the *inipi*, or sweat ceremony. The *inipi* is a ritual of purification that cleanses both the body and the spirit. It takes place inside a small round structure called a sweat lodge. The Lakota traditionally made a sweat lodge of bent saplings, which they covered completely with bison hides. Today they cover the sapling framework with blankets and rugs. The Lakota say that the sweat lodge represents the womb of Mother Earth. It is a comforting place to be.

Near the sweat lodge a fire is built to heat the stones that will be used. The leader of the ritual sits

inside by the entrance with a pail of cold water. Once all the participants are seated inside, the hot stones are passed, one at a time, through the doorway by pitchfork. They are lowered into a small pit dug into the ground in the center of the lodge. The leader sprinkles them with cedar tips, which crackle and fill the lodge with fragrance. When the last stone has been placed in the pit, the entrance flap is lowered. Inside, the sweat lodge is dark, warm, and peaceful.

The leader begins the ritual by singing a prayer song while pouring water over the stones. As the steam rises, the participants join in the song. Each person then offers, in turn, a personal prayer. More songs are sung, and more water is poured over the steaming stones. The participants rub sage over their skin. The sweet smell of sage and cedar mingles with the steam. As the bodies of the participants are cleansed through sweat, their spirits are purified through prayer.

When the ritual has ended, the doorway flap is lifted, letting the cool air drift in. The participants come out of the lodge into the fresh breeze washing over the plains. They now feel uplifted and purified, with all bad feelings left behind.

The sweat ritual may be done alone or with others. It may be done whenever a person is feeling bad emotionally or physically. It may be done regularly as refreshment for the body and the spirit. And, whenever people take part in a ceremony during which the spirits will be present, they must first be purified in the sweat lodge.

Many Native American nations across the continent have sweat rituals. Certain features differ from group to group. For example, different groups make the sweat lodge differently, sometimes covering it with earth or wood instead of blankets and rugs. And the prayers and songs always vary among the different Native nations.

CHAPTER
FOUR

—◉—

SEASONAL
CEREMONIES

Native American peoples have always felt closely tied to the land they live on. The land is more than just a place where they happen to be. It is home, the place given to them by the Creator when people were first made. Many areas are considered sacred places where the spirits dwell and are visited for rituals and prayers.

The land has also provided what the people needed to live. It gave them wood, clay, and other materials for building their homes. It offered wild plants, nuts, and berries for food. It sheltered the animals that the people hunted and fished for. It provided the fertile earth in which seeds could be planted to grow many kinds of crops, including corn, squash, beans, pumpkins, and tobacco.

Native peoples were in tune with the change of seasons. Their survival depended on knowing which times of the year were best for hunting certain animals and gathering wild plants. And the crops they planted would give food only during the growing season. To ignore the rhythm of the seasons would mean facing starvation.

Many Native American ceremonies continue to recognize the people's dependence on the land and on the forces of nature. Each of these ceremonies occurs once a year during a specific season. A seasonal ceremony is a time for all to pray together and honor the spirits as a community. Often an entire village or town will work together to make sure that the ceremony is a success.

THE GREEN CORN DANCE OF THE CREEK

Many Native American societies have traditionally relied on farming as their main source of food. Corn is an especially important crop. In the Eastern Woodlands, farming peoples usually hold a ceremony called the Green Corn Dance or Green Corn Festival. Though details of the ceremony differ from nation to nation, the Green Corn Dance is generally a harvest festival, held in the summer when the corn is ripe. It is a ceremony of thanksgiving and a celebration of the new year. In Oklahoma the various towns of the Creek nation hold their Green Corn Dances in July or August. Today, as in the past, no one may eat any of the new corn before the festival begins.

The Green Corn Dance of the Creek lasts four days. On the first day the town's priest, or fire builder, enters the ceremonial grounds and kindles a fire. His attendants follow carrying pieces of wood, which they add to the fire. Four ears of new corn are then placed on the flames. By giving up these first ears of corn, the

Creek symbolically give back to nature what nature has given to them. It is a way of showing thanks.

Also on the first day, a liquid called the "black drink" is brewed from wild roots that grow in the marshes and prairies. The black drink is an emetic. An emetic is a medicine that, when swallowed, causes a person to vomit. Like the various Native American sweat rituals, this is a ritual of purification. By taking the black drink, the Creek cleanse both their bodies and their spirits.

Throughout the four days of the Green Corn Dance, participants perform several kinds of dances. Among them are the Ribbon Dance, performed by women wearing long streaming ribbons of many colors, and the Feather Dance, in which men carry poles topped with heron feathers. There are also periods of resting and of fasting. Not to eat or drink is considered a personal sacrifice in many Native American ceremonies. In fact, the Green Corn Dance is sometimes called the Busk, which comes from the Creek word *puskita* (or *boskita*), meaning "to fast." But on the last day of the festival a great feast is prepared, and everyone enjoys the new bounty of the harvest.

In the days before electricity, when homes were lighted by fire, the Creek put out all the fires in their towns just before the Green Corn Dance was held. They swept all the hearths clean of ashes. Then they lit new fires with the flames from the fire kindled on the first day of the ceremony. During the ceremony any criminals who joined the activities were pardoned of their crimes. These acts were a symbol of "starting over" in a fresh new year. Today the Green Corn Dance still carries the same meaning. It is a time of starting anew, when past wrongs are forgiven. It is a time of thanking the earth for its harvest and praying for good harvests to come. It is a time of joy, good feelings, and hope for the coming year.

THE SNAKE CEREMONY OF THE HOPI

Rising from the desert in Arizona are three flat-topped mountains called mesas. Atop these mesas stand the villages, or pueblos, of the Hopi people. The Hopi have been farmers for thousands of years. But it is seldom easy to farm in a desert. The climate is often harsh and the weather unpredictable. In order to make sure that their crops continue to grow, the Hopi turn to the supernatural world for help.

From about the end of December to mid-July, the Hopi hold kachina ceremonies. Kachinas are supernatural beings that represent many things, such as plants, animals, thunder, and other forces of nature. They help the Hopi in many ways. One of the most important ways is in helping to bring rain.

The kachina spirits are said to live in the San Francisco peaks that rise near the Hopi villages, but come to live among the Hopi during the ceremonies. At this time Hopi men wear masks and outfits to look like the kachinas. By doing this they take on the personalities of the kachina spirits and are said to become the kachinas themselves. They dance in the village plazas and in the kivas, the underground rooms used only for rituals. Sometimes they give small carved wooden kachina figures to the children. This is a way to help Hopi children learn about the kachinas.

At the end of these ceremonies, the kachina spirits go back to the mountains. Then, from July to December, other ceremonies, without kachinas, are held. One of these ceremonies, usually held in August, is the Snake Ceremony.

By August the summer winds have dried the springs and parched the ground in the Hopi area. Rain at this time is very important for the crops to finish ripening. The Hopi consider snakes to be the people's messengers to the rain beings who live beneath the earth. Snakes move close to the ground, and their movement resembles a zigzag of lightning in the sky.

The Snake Ceremony, held to bring rain, lasts sixteen days. Performed by members of the Snake and Antelope societies, it includes dances, rituals in the kivas, foot races, and the ritual gathering of snakes. Hopi men dance with these snakes during the spectacular Snake Dance, held on the final day of the ceremony.

It takes four days to gather all the snakes. On each of the four days, men of the Snake Society catch as many snakes as they can by looking for the tracks the animals make on the ground when they slither. They catch whichever kinds of snakes they can, including rattle-snakes, bull snakes, and sidewinders.

Each day all the men go out together looking in a different direction—west of the village one day, south another, east another, and finally north. They bring the snakes they catch to the kiva of the Snake Society. There the snakes will be kept in jars and let out now and then to move around while the men in the kiva sing prayer songs.

On the final day of the ceremony, visitors often arrive at the village to watch the Snake Dance. They crowd around the plaza and sit on the flat rooftops of the Hopi houses, waiting for the dance to begin. Inside the plaza a shelter of evergreen branches, called a *kisi*, has been made. In front of it a shallow pit has been dug and a wooden board laid over it. This pit is a symbol of the entrance to the underworld, the place from which the Hopi came long, long ago. The snakes are brought from the kiva and placed inside the *kisi*. Meanwhile, in the kivas members of the Snake and Antelope societies dress and paint their bodies for the dance.

Finally, the dancers enter the plaza. To the sound of rattles, they circle the plaza four times. As they pass the *kisi*, each man stomps on the board that has been placed over the pit, making a deep, powerful sound like thunder. This is a call to the beings below. It tells them that the people above are performing the ceremony.

Each dancer of the Snake Society in turn then goes to the *kisi* and picks up a snake in his mouth. He gently holds the animal with his teeth just below the head, while holding the rest of the animal's body in his hands. Another Snake Society member close beside him strokes the snake with a feather wand to calm it. By holding the snake in his mouth, the dancer gives his prayers straight to the snake messenger.

After all the snakes in the *kisi* have been danced with, the snakes are brought back to the desert and released to the four directions. Now the snakes can take

the prayers of the people back to the supernaturals, and the rain will come.

Each Hopi village across the three mesas holds its Snake Ceremony every two years. In the year the Snake Ceremony is not held, members of the Gray Flute and Blue Flute societies conduct the Flute Ceremony. It includes prayers at the sacred spring, usually dry at this time, and a procession back to the village. This ceremony, too, is performed to bring rain and fill the springs and wells.

CHAPTER FIVE

HEALING RITUALS AND CEREMONIES

A healing ritual sometimes forms part of a larger ceremony, and sometimes it is a ceremony in itself. It is performed when a person is suffering. Usually the patient is physically sick, but sometimes he or she may have a mental or emotional illness or may be experiencing some misfortune. The healing ritual is performed by an individual medicine man or woman or by members of a medicine society.

In Native American tradition, the word *medicine* means more than just something you take to cure your body. It is true that medicine men and women know how to treat the sick by using herbs and other kinds of natural remedies. But, as we have seen, Native Americans do not separate the physical and spiritual worlds. The medicine man or woman must also offer songs and prayers to heal the spirit. This, too, is medicine. It is only by treating both the body and the spirit that a medicine person may truly heal someone.

The Navajo of the Four Corners region of the Southwest are well known for their skill at weaving beautiful rugs and for their exquisite sandpaintings. Many of these sandpaintings are created during curing ceremonies, which include a lot of prayer songs. For this reason, the ceremonies are called chants or sings and the medicine person, usually a man, is called a singer.

For the Navajo the world is a place of natural harmony and beauty. But sometimes something may happen to disturb this harmony and cause disorder in the universe. For example, a person may accidentally displease the supernatural beings, called the Holy Ones. As a result, the person may become sick or meet with misfortune. A chant will restore the person to harmony with the powers of nature and the supernatural, so that she or he will get better.

When a person appears to be ill and no one seems to know the cause, the patient's family will hire a "hand-trembler." The hand-trembler performs a ritual in which he sings prayers and offers corn pollen to the Holy Ones. He places his hands over the body of the patient and a hand will begin to shake, or tremble. The way his hand shakes tells the hand-trembler what type of chant the patient needs.

Each of the many kinds of chants has its own name, such as "Night Way," "Mountaintop Way," and "Enemy Way." Each chant cures a different type of trouble and may last as long as nine days or nights. Hundreds of songs and hundreds of sandpaintings go with a chant. A man who wants to learn a chant must be taught by another singer. It takes many years to learn and memorize the songs and sandpaintings for just one chant, so a singer usually learns only a few chants in his lifetime.

During a chant the singer treats the patient with herbs and natural medicines and creates sandpaintings, also called dry paintings. With help from his assistants, the singer prays and sings as he creates a picture, or "painting." These pictures are made by sprinkling colored "sand" made from crushed minerals, corn pollen, and crushed charcoal on a bed of smooth sand or on buckskin.

Sandpaintings may be as small as 1 or 2 feet (about 0.5 meter) across, or as large as 15 to 20 feet (about 5 to 6 meters) or more. These pictures tell the stories of the Holy Ones. By creating them the singer is calling on the Holy Ones to come and help the patient. It is very important that he do everything just right. If he makes a mistake, the Holy Ones will not recognize the call and they will not come. Then the patient will not be cured.

Because the singer prays and sings over the sandpainting, it becomes a powerful object. The patient is told to sit on the sandpainting as the singer begins the healing. By doing this the patient absorbs all the powerful blessings that have been put into the painting. Because it is so powerful, the painting must be destroyed completely by the end of the day or night that it is created. When the singer finishes healing the patient, the "sand" is gathered up from the painting and either buried or scattered to the four directions.

THE FALSE FACE SOCIETY OF THE IROQUOIS

It is said that in the dense green forests of New York State and southern Ontario, Canada, spirits would sometimes appear to Iroquois hunters. These spirits had long hair that whipped their faces as they darted from tree to tree. They were not harmful spirits. All they wanted from the hunters was some of the tobacco and cornmeal that the hunters carried when they traveled.

The spirits said they had the power to control sickness. They told people to carve their portraits in wood. If people called upon them while wearing the portrait masks, burning tobacco, and singing certain songs, they would give those people the power to cure sickness.

Those who follow this practice belong to a curing society known as the False Face Society. Today, as in the past, an Iroquois who is sick may call upon a member of the False Face Society for healing. People who have been cured by the society or have dreamed of the False Face spirits can become members themselves.

False Face masks are usually made from basswood. They may be made from a block of wood, although the traditional way to make a mask is to carve the face into a living tree. After the carver forms the face, he removes it from the tree and adds the details. The faces often have crooked noses and mouths, or wide puckered lips, sometimes with the tongues sticking out. They usually have long hair and wide staring eyes rimmed with metal. They are made this way because that is how the False Face spirits look.

As a mask maker carves a mask, he prays and burns tobacco as an offering to the spirits. A mask made in this way becomes sacred and powerful. Carving into a living tree helps to give the mask greater strength. The mask is believed to have a life of its own and must always be treated with the greatest respect. When not in use, it must be properly taken care of. It must be oiled and "fed" by burning tobacco and rubbing corn mush on its mouth.

When a False Face Society member puts on the mask and performs the proper ritual using a turtle-shell rattle, the power of the spirits works through him to heal the sick. During this ritual a society member will pick up hot ashes to blow on the patient. He puts his hands into the glowing embers, but he does not get burned because he is protected by the power of the spirits.

Besides performing curing ceremonies, the False Face Society also plays an important role in the Iroquois Midwinter Ceremony. Like the Green Corn Dance of the Creek, the Midwinter Ceremony celebrates a new year. It is a time of starting anew, when members of the False Face Society go to all the houses in town and purify them. The False Face members borrow the power of the spirits to drive out any sickness or misfortune dwelling in the houses. This ritual blesses the Iroquois people and prevents harm from entering their homes.

CHAPTER SIX

POWWOWS

They can happen anywhere—indoors in a civic center or gymnasium, outdoors in a field or public park. Whether held indoors or out, powwows are always colorful and festive events. They may be held by a particular nation, or they may be intertribal, held by various Native nations. Originally a celebration of the Plains nations, the powwow is now hosted by Native peoples from all parts of North America. It is a time when they can come together and share their traditions with one another and with non-Native visitors of all colors, beliefs, and nationalities.

Powwows are often large events that are held annually, like Crow Fair in Montana, Honor the Earth Powwow in Wisconsin, and the Mountain Eagle Indian Festival in upstate New York. They last several days and attract many people, both Native and non-Native. Often people come from far away to attend. If the event is outdoors, many will set up tents and canvas tepees along the fringes of the powwow grounds, where they will remain camped for the festivities. Some will participate in the dance contests. Some will set up tables to sell their merchandise. Others are there just to enjoy the event and to mix with the visitors who have come to watch the dancers and listen to the music.

At the center of the grounds a circle is set up, usually marked off by rope. As the day begins, dancers in bright regalia line up outside the circle waiting for the signal to enter. At one end of the circle is the "drum," a group of people who sit around a large drum and play the songs from various Native nations that the people will dance to. They bring their sticks down hard on the drumhead, producing a loud, powerful sound as their voices carry the chants and songs in their original languages. The dancers enter the circle to begin.

There are different kinds of dances, and each dancer wears a different style of regalia. Although pow-wows are a modern celebration, the dances are similar to dance styles of olden times. Men who dance in the traditional style of warriors often wear clothes of buckskin, with a bustle of feathers attached in back and a hair roach—a stiff brush of deer and porcupine hairs—attached to their heads. Some will wear a breastplate of bone beads covering the chest and reaching down to the thighs. These men dance with stomping motions and the short, alert moves of a warrior listening for the sounds of his enemies.

Younger men often "fancy-dance." Wearing two bustles of brightly colored feathers and clothes of colorful fabric, they hop and twirl, touch the ground with their knees, and jump up again to continue in an energetic swirling motion.

There are "grass dancers" whose bodies jiggle and stomp beneath their regalia of bright cloth and streaming yarn.

There are "jingle dress" dancers, young women whose cloth dresses are decorated with tin cones that jingle with a bright tinkling sound as they move.

Other women dancers are dressed in colorful cloth or buckskin dresses decorated with beautiful designs of beadwork, ribbonwork, or porcupine quillwork. Some dance traditional style, while others, usually younger women and girls, fancy-dance. Traditional dancers carry a fringed shawl folded neatly over one arm and dance with slow, steady steps. Fancy-dancers wear a shawl over their shoulders. When they dance, they stomp and twirl, their shawls moving with the motion of their arms like eagles' wings.

And there are the children, little boys and girls who dress and dance in the tradition of their elders.

As the day continues, the dancers will be judged. Each dancer has a number and may win prize money if he or she is judged best. But there are other dances, too, performed just for fun: line dances, partner dances, and circle dances. Also important is the Veterans' Dance, in which men and women who have fought in wars are honored for their courage.

Meanwhile, vendors sell their merchandise from tables set up a short distance from the circle. Here visitors can purchase baskets and pottery, clothing and pouches of finely decorated leather and fur, bark containers, jewelry of silver or beadwork, tapes of Native music, books, artwork, and food.

When the dancing stops for intermissions during the day, special performances may take place. Native peoples from Central and South America are sometimes invited to share their traditions through music and dance. Storytellers enter the circle to tell tales of tricksters, spirits, and marvelous happenings. Flutists play the traditional Native American courting flute.

Sometimes at a powwow, as on other occasions, a family may host a "giveaway." This is a ritual of the Plains nations that is held to honor a person, such as a soldier returning from war, a student graduating from college, or a child receiving a name. To celebrate the occasion the honored person's family will give away gifts to all the people present.

At a powwow there is excitement in the air. People are happy, calm, and relaxed. The day is filled with the sound of the drum and the movement of the dancers, as the fragrance of corn soup and fry bread rises from the pots beneath the awnings. This is a time of lightheartedness and goodwill. Powwows are a time to celebrate being a Native American.

CHAPTER SEVEN

CONTINUING TRADITIONS

We have explored only a few of the many powerful ceremonies of Native American peoples. But Native peoples have not always enjoyed the freedom to practice their rituals and ceremonies openly. Government policies have often disrupted the lifeways of Native peoples and interfered with many of their customs and traditions. As Europeans began to settle the land, Native peoples were often forced to move from their original homelands to places far away. Others found that their lands were getting smaller and smaller.

By the end of the nineteenth century, reservations had been established in the United States, and reserves in Canada. The governments of both countries tried to force Native peoples to give up their traditional lifeways and adopt the lifestyles of white society, including Christianity. Native children were sent to boarding schools far away. Once there, the children were not allowed to wear their hair long or wear traditional clothing. If they spoke their Native languages, they were punished.

In both the United States and Canada, Native American religious practices were outlawed for many years. People who were found taking part in traditional rituals or ceremonies were punished and their ceremonial objects seized. Nevertheless, many people still held their rituals in secret. Today, these important events are no longer outlawed.

Not all Native peoples practice traditional rituals. Some are Christians. Others have combined traditional ways with Christianity. But for those who choose to follow traditional religious practices, certain problems remain.

For example, some rituals must be conducted in sacred areas where the spirits dwell. But many of these places are now public parks. Because they must share these places with hikers and campers, Native people often cannot perform their rituals properly. Some rituals require the use of certain wild plants and animals, but government rules often forbid gathering plants in public parks and hunting animals out of season. Sacred areas are sometimes changed or destroyed by construction, such as the building of dams and roads, and can no longer be used for rituals.

There are other problems, too. Native American burial places are often dug up by archaeologists who wish to study the human bones and objects found in the graves. For many Native peoples this is an offensive and disrespectful act. And some rituals require certain objects that are now in museums and not available for use.

In 1978 Congress passed the American Indian Religious Freedom Act (AIRFA) to help Native peoples protect their religious beliefs. But the act often does not protect religious practices. The AIRFA is used in court cases as an aid to Native peoples. Some of these cases have been won, but the battle for religious freedom continues.

Native peoples still face other hardships, too, including poverty, health problems, and unemployment. In spite of these difficulties, Native American traditions continue. Rituals and celebrations are among the most important of these traditions. They are ways for the people to bond with one another and share a common identity. They help the people to deal better with their problems by giving them strength when times are hard.

Though some parts of these rituals and ceremonies have changed in certain ways, change does not mean destruction. No human society remains the same forever. Each must move forward as changing times demand. Native American societies are no exception.

Native peoples have done more than just survive their difficult history. They have kept their customs, their languages, their stories, and their arts alive from generation to generation. In spite of opposition, they have kept the things that are most important to them. These they carry with them into the future.

ACTIVITIES

NATIVE AMERICAN RECIPES, CRAFTS, AND GAMES

RECIPES

North America is a land rich in a variety of wild plants, berries, roots, and nuts. These foods have been harvested from the earth by Native American women for thousands of years. Many Native societies also relied heavily on farm crops, especially corn, beans, and squash, for their main sources of food.

Many of the dishes we eat today were originally prepared by Native peoples long before they came in contact with Europeans. For example, corn on the cob, baked beans, and clam chowder are all Native American dishes. Today, as in the past, feasting on traditional foods is still an important feature of Native American celebrations.

CORN SOUP

Ingredients

- *¼ pound stewing beef*
- *oil*
- *4 cups water*
- *1 small onion, chopped*
- *1 cup corn kernels*
- *1 package beef broth*

Cut the beef into 1-inch cubes and brown them in oil in a skillet. Add the water to a medium-size saucepan along with the chopped onion, the corn, and the beef broth. When the meat is browned, add it to the other ingredients. Bring the mixture to a boil. Then lower the heat, cover the pot, and let it simmer for about an hour, stirring occasionally. This recipe serves four people.

FRY BREAD

Ingredients

- *oil*
- *3 cups flour*
- *1 tablespoon baking powder*
- *1 teaspoon salt*
- *water*

Ask an adult to help you make this deep-fried quick bread.

Fill a medium-size saucepan halfway to the top with oil. Heat the oil slowly on low heat. Meanwhile, in a large bowl, combine the flour, baking powder, and salt, and add enough water to make a soft dough. Mix the dough with a spoon until all the lumps are gone.

Form the dough into 3-inch balls and place the balls on waxed paper dusted with flour. To keep the dough from sticking to your hands, coat your hands lightly with flour. Flatten each ball into a thin round sheet and use a long-handled fork to carefully lower it into the oil. Let the dough cook until it becomes golden brown, turning it over with a fork once so that both sides can cook.

As each sheet of bread is finished, remove it with a fork and place it on a paper towel to soak up the extra oil. This recipe makes about five breads.

Fry bread may be eaten as a sweet or taco-style. For sweet fry bread, top with powdered sugar or honey. For taco-style, top with cooked chopped meat, chopped tomatoes, shredded lettuce, shredded cheddar cheese, and taco sauce.

Native American artists create beautifully crafted products, including corn husk dolls and delicate quillwork boxes that are often sold as art objects or displayed in art galleries.

As we have seen from certain rituals, corn has always been an important food for many Native American peoples. It also provides natural materials for making things. The husk of the corn, the outside covering, has been used to make a variety of objects, including masks, mats, and salt bottles. Iroquois women also used corn husk to make dolls for children to play with.

CORN HUSK DOLLS

Materials

- *package of corn husk*
  (Corn husk may be purchased at most craft shops. Each package makes several dolls.)
- *pan of warm water*
- *china or glass plate*
- *scissors*

To make a corn husk figure, you must first soak the husks. Separate the husks in the pan of warm water and allow them to soak for at least an hour. Because the husks are light, some will float to the surface and will not become properly soaked. You can keep them under water by placing a plate over them in the pan. The weight of the plate will keep them down.

After the husks have been soaked, choose five pieces. They will be used as follows:

- *Husk 1 = head, neck, wrists, and ankles*
- *Husk 2 = body*
- *Husk 3 = arms*
- *Husk 4 = shoulders*
- *Husk 5 = waist*

Tear a strip (about one quarter of the husk) from husk 1 and crumple it into a ball. This will be the doll's head. Place this ball in the center of husk 2. Bring husk 2 over the ball and tie it off with another thin strip torn from husk 1. This forms the neck.

Roll up husk 3 lengthwise as you would roll up a rug. This will be the doll's arms. Using strips from husk 1, tie off the doll's wrists near the end of each side. Place this roll between the two flaps of the doll's body just below the head.

Split husk 4 in half. Use one strip to form one shoulder. Use the other to form the other shoulder. They should cross at the waist. Fold husk 5 in half and tie it around the doll's waist where the strips that form the shoulders meet.

Using the scissors, trim the bottom of the husk that forms the doll's dress. For a boy doll, separate the bottom portion of the husk below the waist and tie off ankles to form legs.

Traditionally, corn husk dolls did not have faces. If you like, you may paint a face on your doll and make clothing out of scraps of material.

QUILLED BOX   Eastern Woodlands peoples often made containers of tree bark, especially the bark of the birch tree. They sometimes used these containers as cooking pots, as well as to store and gather food and to store personal items.

Often, birchbark containers were beautifully decorated with designs made by etching through bark stencils. The Micmac of Nova Scotia, Canada, often decorated their bark containers with fancy designs made of brightly dyed porcupine quills. Over time, the technique of quilling boxes spread to other Woodlands peoples. Today these items can still be purchased at powwows and stores carrying Native American art.

Although quilling boxes is an art that must be learned, you can do a similar activity.

Materials

- *cardboard box*
- *porcupine quills*
  (These may be purchased at craft stores carrying Native American materials.)
- *food coloring*
  (several bottles of different colors)
- *clear-drying glue*
- *scissors*

Choose a box whose size and shape you like, such as a small gift box or an oatmeal container. Soak the porcupine quills in the food coloring and allow them to dry on a paper towel. When the quills are dry, glue them to the

surface of the box or container, creating your own design. Trim the quills with the scissors wherever necessary before gluing.

GAMES

Native American children and adults have long enjoyed a wide variety of games. These include games of speed and skill, such as foot races and ball games, and games of chance, such as guessing games and dice. Most of these games were played across North America, although the rules varied among the different groups and the game equipment was made differently. Although some games were played for amusement, adult sports were usually an important part of ceremonies and festivals, as they often are today.

BALL AND STICK RACES

Ball and stick races were especially popular among Native peoples of the Southwest. Two racers or two teams of racers competed by kicking a ball or stick around a course before returning to the place they started from. Balls were often made of wood, stone, tree resin, or animal hide stuffed with plant fiber or fur. Sticks were usually of wood or bone, and sometimes a ring of twig or plant fiber was used in place of a ball or stick. Courses were usually many miles wide. Sometimes the race covered a distance of 25 miles (40 kilometers).

You can play a version of this race using either a short stick or a small rubber ball. Choose a flat piece of ground, such as a playground, schoolyard, or empty lot. If more than two people want to participate, choose sides and team up. One player from each team races at a time.

Decide on a starting place. Begin there and kick the ball or stick around the edge of the yard until you return to the starting place. Or you can kick the ball or stick in a straight line to the other end of the yard and back again. Any player who touches the stick or ball with his or her hands is disqualified. The person who returns first is the winner. If you are playing on teams, the team that has the most victories after everyone has had a turn is the winning team.

THE MOCCASIN GAME

The Moccasin Game is a type of guessing game. It was played by hiding a small object, such as a stone or bullet, under a moccasin or container, such as a wooden cup or cane tube. At each game there were usually four moccasins or containers. The player skillfully placed his or her hand beneath each but left the object under only one, and the opponent had to guess which one. Sometimes more than one object was hidden, but one of them was marked. The player placed an object under each moccasin or container, and the opponent had to guess under which one the marked object was hidden.

Sticks or beans were usually used as counters to keep score. As the game was being played, the people watching often sang or shouted and made noise. This was done to keep the opponent from concentrating, and it added excitement to the game.

To play your own version of the Moccasin Game, you will need one other person and the following materials:

- *20 sticks or twigs*
- *4 plastic drinking cups*
- *1–4 pebbles*
  (You may substitute drinking straws or beans for sticks, and shells or buttons for pebbles.)

Divide the sticks into two equal piles. Each person takes one pile. These are your counters to help you keep score.

On either a table or the floor, place the cups in a line in front of you. Take a pebble in your hand and be sure to keep it hidden as you lift each cup and pretend to place the pebble underneath it. You may lift the cups as many times as you like. When you are ready, ask your opponent where the pebble is hidden.

For a more challenging game, use four pebbles and mark one with a felt-tip marker. Keep all four pebbles hidden in your hand as you lift the cups, but place only one under each cup. Your opponent must guess where the marked pebble is hidden.

Speed helps in this game. Your opponent will find it harder to guess if you are quick in lifting the cups and in moving your hands underneath them.

For each correct guess, a player gets a counter from his or her opponent. A player continues to guess until he or she guesses wrong. Then it is the other player's turn to guess. The two players switch back and forth between hiding and guessing until one player wins all the counters.

butte: a hill or mountain standing alone

celebration: a festive occasion

ceremony: a formal act or series of acts that may mark a happy event, like a birth or marriage, or a crisis, like an illness or the need for rain

emetic: a medicine that, when swallowed, causes a person to vomit

False Face Society: a medicine society of the Iroquois

fast: a period of time when a person does not eat

festival: a time of celebration

gan: Apache mountain spirits

Hamatsa Society: a secret society of the Kwakiutl

inipi: a Lakota ceremony of purification

initiation: a time when a person moves from one stage of life into another, as when a child becomes an adult

kachinas: Hopi spirits that represent many things, such as plants, animals, and thunder and other forces of nature *kisi*: the shelter where the snakes are kept during the Hopi Snake Dance

kiva: an underground room used by the Hopi for rituals

mesa: a flat-topped mountain

potlatch: a ceremony of the Northwest Coast peoples that includes feasting, speeches, the performance of dramas, and the giving of gifts

puberty: the time when a boy's or girl's body begins to physically change into that of a man or woman (about twelve to fourteen years old)

puskita: a Creek word that means "to fast"

regalia: traditional Native American clothing worn on special occasions

rite: a kind of ritual

ritual: a set of actions that follows the same pattern, usually for a special event or reason

sacred: deserving the highest respect, usually linked to a people's religious beliefs

tradition: a custom that is passed from generation to generation

FOR FURTHER READING

Ancona, George. *Powwow*. San Diego, New York, London: Harcourt Brace Jovanovich, 1993.

Bruchac, Joseph, and Jonathan London. *Thirteen Moons on Turtle's Back: A Native American Year of Moons*. Illustrated by Thomas Locker. New York: Philomel Books, 1992.

Hirschfelder, Arlene B., and Beverly R. Singer, eds. *Rising Voices: Writings of Young Native Americans*. New York: Scribner's, 1992.

Ortiz, Simon. *The People Shall Continue*. Illustrated by Sharol Graves. San Francisco: Childrens Book Press, 1988.

Sneve, Virginia Driving Hawk, ed. *Dancing Teepees: Poems of American Indian Youth*. Illustrated by Stephen Gammell. New York: Holiday House, 1989.

INDEX

ABOUT THE AUTHOR

As a senior museum instructor at the American Museum of Natural History in New York City, Lisa Sita develops programs that present a range of anthropology topics to children and adults. She was previously associated with the Museum of the American Indian in New York and holds undergraduate and master's degrees in anthropology. Native American culture has long been her special focus, and she has made repeated visits to the Rosebud Reservation in South Dakota to deepen her knowledge and understanding of Lakota Sioux society and traditions. Her articles have appeared in *Faces* magazine and other publications; this is her first book.